Inhale Exhale
...and live!

Maria Alexandra Zaharia

BookLeaf Publishing

Presentation by *BookLeaf Publishing*

Web: www.bookleafpub.com

E-mail: info@bookleafpub.com

ISBN: 9789357211703

First edition 2023

DEDICATION

To the ones I love most

May this be worthy of their eyes

ACKNOWLEDGEMENT

Special thanks go to my mum and my grandmother for having an immeasurable amount of trust in me and for being my biggest cheerleaders; my partner for all of the late night advice, reassurance and encouragement throughout this labour of love; and the rest of my family for ultimately believing in me and what I could achieve. Finally, I would also like to show my appreciation to Mother Nature for all of the inspiration it has provided me with.

PREFACE

Inhale Exhale ...and live! came from a personal desire to inject some decisiveness and bring some continuity into all of the breathing in and out we are being advised to try out these days. I have always felt as if, whilst deep respirations might initially help whenever feeling overwhelmed, these also had to be followed by some action or reaction which would demonstrate that we were putting the advice to good use. Staying alive resonated with the current version of myself, and so I felt as if this would be a clear-cut end goal that could follow our respirations. It took me 27 days to complete the first draft and just as long to feel brave enough to submit it, but I am now so glad I did!

The Author
London, 2022

Audiovisual

The distant murmuring
Of a sudden rainstorm,
Its tapping against
A steamed up window:
Blank canvas for mindless doodling

In the background
An episode of a popular sitcom
Running on the telly
Bright and flashy images
Accompanied by a brassy laugh track

The glossy feathers
And repetitive squawks
Of a well-dressed
But insistent magpie
Good morning general!

The kettle finally reaching
Its boiling point
The tea leaves' soft sigh
As the water embraces them
One cheeky sip of this relaxing cuppa
Enough to blur your lenses up

That song you heard last night
On the way back
You thought to yourself
"Now this is going to

Get stuck with me forever!"
How did it go again?

Just anything to keep
Any intrusive thoughts
At bay

Let all of it sink in
And wash over you
Inhale
Exhale
...and live!

Self-reflection

They say that
One's eyes
Are the mirror
To their very soul
Yet never explain
Why one's
Own vision
Frequently betrays them
Of how
Introspection
Is such a valuable
Complex concept
To grasp
That one often
Feels compelled to
Use their own words
To conceal
What they are
Actually feeling

lunar

Reigning o'er the dark

cold disc of polished silver

Gently glides aloft

then plunges into water

—splash! the mirror is shattered

stellar

the night sky's freckles

most humans wish upon these

only when they fall

solar

6

At the break of dawn

when the whole world arises

and begins anew

Arrows made of solid gold

rip through the candy floss clouds

TGIF?

Pleasantly cushioned by the glee
And bliss of the weekend
It's none other than Friday, the
Day on which all depend!

We're thinking of this all week long
Summon it, unconstrained
It is the hope that keeps us strong
When we are feeling drained.

But, in our rushing, we forget
To stop and take our time
Then, in hindsight, there's much regret
That is not worth a dime.

So, whilst I hope that your Fridays
Are brighter than the Sun,
Don't wish away the other days—
Instead, treasure each one!

Metempsychosis

When you left
You took with you
A piece of myself

In its place
A numb and hollow gap
Remained

A void
Devoid of feeling
Or emotion

I tried to fill
The emptiness
With just about anything

For the longest time
Nothing
Would suffice

Your presence no longer
Inhabited the places
You'd once occupied

Then suddenly
I started seeing you
In the colours of the rainbow

Each droplet of rain
Would be a tear
I no longer had to shed

I began hearing
Your laughter
With every gust of wind

And each ray of sunshine
Would carry some
Of your warmth with it

I realised
You'd become
Immortal and endless

That you were now
A part of life's
Greatest wonders

And that, to conjure you,
I'll have to carry on
Making the most out of these

joy

10

an elusive word

fragile, yet its value:

inestimable

The butterfly effect

You might not believe it, but one of the things
Capable of moving mountains, heaven and earth
Is but the flutter of a psyche's paper-thin wings—
The briefest of motions, for all that is worth!

Often overlooked, or wholly disregarded,
Its rippling effect can surely cause quite a stir
That'll grow even fiercer whenever left unguarded,
Turn into a tornado, some theorists would concur!

As luck would have it, such marvellous forces
Also happen to dwell in and within the self!
They light up our fervour, the brightest of torches,
They stop us from keeping ourselves on the shelf.

The feeblest of impulses you ought to try unearth!
Start by acknowledging any meek inner movement
Then seek to harness them for your self-improvement
So that you are ready to inherit the earth.

All aboard!

The next train to arrive at
Platform 1
Is the 11:11
Transcendental service to
Every single one of us' purpose

Calling at
Each of life's
Triumphs and laments
Hellos and farewells
Trials and tribulations

This train is formed of
Countless coaches

Please ignore
The call of the void and
Mind the gap
Between the train
And the platform

Procrastination

13

There is a young woman - that's me!
On most days, I would guarantee
That there is still time
To try make this rhyme
At least to a certain degree.

Grounded

You are a creature of habit
A mere mortal, some would think.
Yet, deep inside of you, there lies
Dormant an astounding spark of...
Otherness? Perhaps that isn't quite
What you would like to hear
But it's the truth, nonetheless.

You are minuscule when first born
Only but a seedling, though
The above-mentioned unique flicker is
Since then, profoundly embedded within, Immovable
and beyond recall!
A fatal diagnosis that you cannot
Escape, as fate has thrusted it upon you.

You are slow to grow into your stem,
A shiny, flimsy wrapper but one that
Shields you, helps you fit in, even
Acts as storage for your emotional baggage
And supports each and every accessory
You might amass throughout your lifetime.

You are barely able to survive
Without your leaves, their nervures
Mapping out your vulnerability.
Your thirst is quenched by
The dawn's first droplets of dew

You are nurtured and caressed
By the warmest of lights, the Sun.

You are one of a kind, just know
That once you've finally managed
To put down sturdy roots, well,
Only then you can allow yourself
At long last, to bloom.

lullaby

Surrounded by the

nursery's powdery scent

and mother's sweet voice

Entering the realm of dreams

cradled in the safest of arms

Capital

Let's paint the city red!
Or, to be more precise,
Pantone 485C!

Starting with the pillar boxes,
Then the phone booths
And the double-deckers.
The Central line,
Royal guards' and
Beefeaters' uniforms.
Paddington's bucket hat
Plus his shiny wellies.

Let's tint all of these and more
With that vivid shade
Then call the resulting
Work of art
A mercurial behemoth
Or, simpler yet,
London.

Petrichor

Rat-a-tat, the sound that raindrops make
As they hit the ground, tap dancing together
In mesmerising sync; yet make no mistake
Not many are thrilled by this type of weather!
Downpours succeed harmless sprinkles,
Rattling rooftops and vast, leaden skies,
Or least until these subside into drizzles
Peaceful patters signalling their demise
Scent of earth's richness remaining behind.

Homesick

Home is where our hearts are
Or, at least,
That's what we tell ourselves
To make the longing a tad more bearable

The truth is
Our countries and our yearning for them
Have both been given lodging
Within our atria and ventricles

Each heartbeat is a knock at one of
Memory's various locked doors,
A painful reminder of what we've
Left behind

On some days, reminiscences of our birthplaces
Might cloud up our minds, making it difficult
To focus on
Anything but the raw emotions they stir up

On other occasions, it'll surely seem
Much easier
To write off any nagging feelings
Until we get an unexpected wake-up call

Could be in
For a rude awakening once we finally face
The passing of time's cruel inevitability

And the toll this takes on those we hold dear

Let's try and go back, whenever we have
The chance to do so, cherish such moments, and
Be an entity that proudly represents their heritage,
Even from afar

Let's learn to accept the paradoxical nature
Of leaving our hearts back home and
Actually living
Wherever our hearts have decided to settle down

ROYGBIV (I)

21

a silken ribbon—

made of both rain and light, and

arched over the sky

ROYGBIV (II)

symbol of hope, against

the clouds its message clear:

bent, yet unbroken

Anniversary

Behold, another prospect to celebrate your birth
Illuminated by scores of candles, filled with mirth
Rosy cheeks, thick dollop of icing atop your nose
Together with all those you would consider close
Hear the singing cease, blow off the lights, rejoice
Do still make a wish, but please don't give it voice
Another of Earth's orbits round the Sun, surprise:
You're older by a year, yet stronger and so wise!

Pick and choose

24

I might be the sum
Of my own choices
But they are also
The sum of me—
Better or worse,
Richer or poorer,
Whilst on the
Highest cusp
Of success
Or having just
Hit rock bottom
They might define me
But I am their maker
So what's it gonna be?

Farewell

25

There is this young woman - 'tis I!
Who finds it hard to say goodbye
I'd much rather dash
And make a huge splash
So that I'll go out on a high!

www.ingramcontent.com/pod-product-compliance
Lightning Source LLC
LaVergne TN
LVHW021341200726
843509LV00014B/2617